For the Love of God

Neil Harrison

STEPHEN F AUSTIN STATE UNIVERSITY PRESS

Front Cover Art: Neil Harrison, The Happy Dog, acrylic on canvas, 2022
Author Photo: Kathleen Donnelly

IBSN: 978-1-62288-954-9
For more information:
Stephen F. Austin State University Press
P.O. Box 13007 SFA Station
Nacogdoches, Texas 75962
sfapress@sfasu.edu
www.sfasu.edu/sfapress
936-468-1078
Distributed by Texas A&M University Press Consortium
www.tamupress.com

ACKNOWLEDGMENTS

Grateful acknowledgement to the editors of the following
publications where some of these poems first appeared:
*Black Star Press, Bridge Burner's Publishing, Flyway, Logan House Press,
Lone Willow Press, Midwest Quarterly, Nebraska Life, The Nebraska
Review, Owen Wister Review, Pinyon Review, Pinyon Publishing, Platte
Valley Review, South Dakota Review, Sandhills Press.*

My thanks to members of the various writing groups I've been part
of over the years, and to Kimberly Verhines and Michael Andrews
at Stephen F. Austin State University Press for your work in
publishing this collection.

For the dogs I have known, and to the inscrutable Entity that
designed them. Some call it God; others, the evolutionary process
of Nature. Both are finally futile attempts to comprehend, by
severely limiting, something incomprehensible to the rational mind,
a boundless enigma that can never be accurately conveyed via the
words or the theoretical concepts of human beings. Though it can
be perceived by those whose hearts remain open enough to feel and
accept the eternal mystery of Love.

CONTENTS

Naming Dogs: Intrusions of Memory in 20 Sonnets

Other Dogs

The Happy Dog

The Gypsy

The Gypsy

She was a stray brown pup
found along the highway
and brought to a vet
who gave her to me.

For seventeen years
I shared adventures
with that brown-eyed enigma.
Then they came to an end.

And I understood at last
what she'd been so long teaching,
this love for which
there will be no end.

Roofing the Shed

Up the ladder and onto the shed,
I dropped the bundle on the roof,
took up a shingle, and was nailing it down
when I glanced to my left and saw
Gypsy, just a pup, watching me
from the top of the ladder.

Stay, I told her, as I eased over
and lifted her onto the roof,
shaking my head and wondering
how she'd managed to learn such
a climb, simply by watching me.

I finished nailing the shingle,
then carried her back down the ladder
and watched as she trotted off
in search of further adventures
with my sister's dogs.

Drahthaar

Burr-comb and brush in a coat pocket,
I fall in behind that busy nose
steering her sure as some siren-song
into islands of burdock and cocklebur.

In time, vision-impaired with seed-heads
matting her beard and eyebrows,
she furls her sails, lowers her head
and starts rooting about, trying to get them off.

Once we work out the worst of the tangles,
she stands, shakes hard, then takes off again,
wooly captain drawn toward some new siren,
and what's a mere swabbie to do but sail along.

Best of Friends

Out of the army, I was back in Nebraska,
fishing the Elkhorn with my brother,
our pups racing each other along the sandbars.
My skinny Drahthaar would sprint away
until Joel's Lab-Husky caught up alongside,
then Gypsy would drop her near shoulder,
swing low into Aries, and he'd over, up
and after her, a game they'd carry on
for hours, keeping us all entertained.

Rapture

The second Tuesday of each month
the city's civil defense sirens
sound the voice of impending doom,
and my Drahthaar rockets off the couch,
tips her bearded muzzle to the heavens
and joins the neighborhood pack,
each ecstatic member adding
another link to Darwin's chain.

One dozen sacred days each year
when the sirens wail all over town
and those canine trumpets answer,
the hair rises on the back of my neck
as the fragile walls of time come down
all the way back to the genesis.

Breaking the Ice

All at once that mid-March morning
she was in instead of on the river,
the fast-flowing water threatening
to sweep her downstream and under
the shelf of ice that kept breaking off
each time she tried to pull herself out,
her splayed front paws grasping at nothing
until she turned and faced the current,
swimming hard but going nowhere
as the crust of ice shattered under my feet,
and belly-deep in the frigid water
I carried her out of the Elkhorn, then knelt
in the sand on the bank where I embraced
the warmth of all I could never replace.

River of Dreams

South of Hay Springs, summer of '89,
I slid a canoe into the Niobrara
and drifted east with my Drahthaar, the Gypsy.

We rode wild rapids, overturned at a falls,
weathered dehydration and a violent storm,
found where the river disappears underground.

From our last camp, beneath the highway bridge
south of Springview, we watched the sun set
over a doe and twin fawns in the shallows.

Mid-night, the roar of a semi overhead
rattled me up from a dream of a man
calling out, My face! It's gone!

Just a dream, I shrugged, though inside I knew
what some might expect when they saw me again
had left their world and would not return.

This Long Spring
for Paul

Odd, the way things come together, thoughts of Blake,
his contraries, the scent of lilacs and new-mown grass
on this warm morning, the 7ᵗʰ of June, at the door
to the church and another season, another dark wedding
of heaven and hell, farewell to a mental traveler.

Three weeks ago you asked my plans, up at the lake
where we both ran, and I told you I'd be fishing,
the carp were moving in to spawn. You were going
back on the road, make the long hauls for summer cash.

In the shallow bog they call Spring Lakes, big fish cruising
the tepid water, I watch a boy cock a home-made spear
and thrust into the soft mud. "Aim lower," I tell him,
like my uncle told me before the weight of his years
left him too weak to wade. "They're deeper than they look."

Watching Joe stalk carp with a spear, it's like watching
myself from a long way off. I know we'll never grow
tired of this, just too worn out to carry on.

The bullet's effect was immediate, separating brain and spine.
She stiffened and then fell just as she'd stood, letting go
the cumulative pain of all the years I couldn't lift her out of.

The grave finished, I walked to the river a half mile down
from where she once fell through the ice and I went after,
crashing through the ice and thrusting against the current
to where she was patiently swimming in place.
We shivered together when I carried her out.

10

I dream of ice, and fish, and fire—of seventeen years
with a small brown friend, of a boy with a fishing spear
pulsing in his hands, of fighting sleep on the long haul
through a black night in Montana, your sudden slip
into that false dawn, truck and trucker going over,
over and over, in this long spring of long goodbyes.

Saluting Hawks

Headed toward Valentine, our annual hunt
in the Sandhills southwest of Crookston,
my brother smiled and give a subtle wave
as we drove past a hawk in a cottonwood.

That summer he'd found his ten-year-old
Lab/Husky cross dead in the road,
hit by a car, or more likely a pickup
out where he lived at the time.

When I'd asked afterward where his dog was,
he'd shrugged, then told me where he'd buried
the closest companion he'd had from the time
Aries had been a pocket-size pup.

Driving west that day, for every hawk
he saw hovering, at rest on a post
or in some dead tree along the highway,
I saw that subdued smile and wave.

Eventually I saw more, my brother walking out
to the road that morning, a hawk slowly rising,
like the spirit of a man's best friend, perhaps,
having waited for him through the night.

The Picture in My Hand

Leaving the ground again,
a lean brown dog is rising
over December bluestem,
held mid-leap forever
in the picture in my hand.

Climbing into a blue sky
wide as her boundless heart,
this time going up farther
and faster than I can follow,

pursuing something higher
than the late-rising ringneck
she flushed from head-high grass
that autumn afternoon.

Now, in the picture in my mind,
held mid-leap forever
over December bluestem,
a lean brown dog is rising,
leaving the ground again.

Smokie

Smoke

No camera quick enough to record it,
no words for colors deep enough to paint
the grasses, yuccas, scattered flowers,
that bottomless blue beyond the lone
sharptail folding at the shot and falling
toward a rise across that span where
a blur of fur launches itself and
suddenly it all makes sense—
bird falling, dog mid-leap, your heart
beating wild as the earth beneath
the paws of one of her predators
homing in on one of her prey—
a flash out of nowhere, gone like that,
too quick in every sense for a camera,
and far too full for a thousand words.

Strange Familiar

The car door opens and she's off,
perusing another chapter of the world,
nose to the earth, reading whatever
wrote itself down the nearest trail,

this strange, familiar animal,
wire-hair gray as old pages
bound between German-chocolate covers,
her inquisitive head and quivering tail.

She trots through a cottonwood shelterbelt,
a stand of bluestem, patch of cocklebur,
bounds through tangled Canary grass
and dog-tracks across a bar to the water,

wades in, flops down on her belly,
laps her fill and leaps to her feet,
shakes hard, and a sudden mist
arrays her in Loup River silver.

Smoke (no mirrors)

The first day of school after summer break,
it's no real surprise when he comes home to find
the sofa cushions strewn about the living room floor—
his dog Smoke's a wire-haired pointer
and they tend to be wired pretty tight.

But the second day there's a dozen magazines
spread in a circle on the living room rug
where it appears some renowned historian
might have just stepped out for a well-earned break
after a long afternoon of intense research.

His high-strung historian out in the yard,
he kneels to re-rack Nebraska Life
and finish his chocolate Moo-Latte.
Then he lets her well-read butt back in
so she can lick the cup while he tries a nap.

But the nap's interrupted by a loud thumping
as she tosses her various toys about, and
he thinks she's probably right—it's been
over a year since his knee went out—about time
they got back to jogging after school.

In his running shoes and dressed for action,
he does a few stretches before the short drive west,
out to the bike trail along the river,
where they come upon a speed-texting sleep-walker
who passes by without noticing them.

Then, in the distance, a woman jogging
behind a medium-sized black-and-white dog
with a strange trot, and when they near
he says, "Looks like your dog's limping a little."
She smiles. "He's only got three legs."

And close enough now, he can see it-
her sleek dog has just one hind leg.
"Hit by a car," she says as she passes.
"He sure runs good that way," he calls.
She nods and adds, "Still outruns me."

A little farther on he unsnaps the leash
and they're off, across the trestle over the river
and down the long bike trail between fencerows
ripe with plums, grapes, sunflowers, coneflowers,
and beyond, vast fields of corn and beans.

Across little bridges over nameless creeks,
west three miles to the feedlot corner,
then around and back to the river,
where Smoke heads down for a drink
while he looks on from the trestle.

She swims out into the channel,
then swings around and tries to swim upstream.
He shakes his head, signals her to turn
and go with the current, but she keeps on
paddling against it, getting nowhere.

So he comes off the trestle and calls her
to follow as he heads downstream,
but she snags an exposed piece of rip-rap,
pulls herself onto that precarious perch,
and without so much as a look downriver,

lunges hard-headed straight at the bank,
gains a foothold and slowly emerges,
bedraggled Aphrodite shaking off the foam.
She wags her tail, and he wags his head
as he follows her back to the car.

Pointing Her West

We're barely out of town heading west
but already she knows we're after grouse,
whining and wagging in the passenger seat,
then stomping that handy throttle, my knee,
and staring ahead as though she knows
the full weight of a wirehaired pointer
will get us there faster than any otherwise.

I push her butt back down on the seat, but
her front paws rebound onto the dash
and I shrug, speed on, and rest assured
that this, my wild and wooly compadre,
will whine and wiggle the whole way west,
as full of righteous song and dance
as any decent dashboard Jesus.

On the Elkhorn, September 2000

As we cross a bar a quarter mile wide
my dog locks up in a sudden point.
Nostrils flared, tail aquiver, she stares
toward a ridge of oaks across the river
where I can hear distant squirrels chatter.

I call, but she simply cocks her head,
and all at once I can feel it too,
faint as a breath on the back of my neck,
soft but ominous as summer thunder,
a cloud coming over us on black-tipped wings.

In this bend where the river curls east again
after carving the cliffs we call Yellowbanks,
I stand with my dog staring up in awe
at a staggered line in mass migration
the likes of which I've never seen before.

I rough-count by tens and estimate
they must be half a thousand pelicans
drifting silent overhead, a down river
fading in the east until this daylight dream
releases its hold, and I can breathe again.

Degrees of Bastardy

Under a mare's-tail wisp of cloud,
the noon sky's only adjective,
a robin lands on a yellowing branch
in the oak the experts say needs iron,
and I don't doubt their diagnosis,
but that's a project for another day.

Right now I'm running electric wire
through insulators attached to steel stakes
atop my backyard chain-link fence
to keep Smoke from going AWOL
like she's done too many times before.

And doubtless I'm approaching bastard-hood,
but I figure a jolt or two and she'll stay in,
not end up another hapless casualty
on the highway half a block west of here,
passersby shaking their heads at the certified
bastard who couldn't keep her off the road.

Holy Rolling Smoke, Batman

Yes, Robin, once again, happy as a pig in shh-
uhh let's say happy as a rolling pin in dough,
my dog Smoke's out there on her back,
scooting through a pile of maple leaves,
rubbing October into her wire-haired hide
deep enough to haul a fair helping of the season
back into the bat-cave to share with me,
mud tracked all across the floors each spring,
dirt and grass from her diggings all summer,
a good lord's wealth of autumn leaves,
and enough fresh-fallen snow each winter
to pretty well house a snowshoe hare,
though she sure ain't much for cleaning up after—
and where in hell's Alfred when you need him?

Bath-Time for Smokie

Shampoo at the ready, I roll up my pants,
doff shoes and socks, then turn on the water,
and knuckles white around her collar,
reach for the garden hose.

Time to tackle that wild-dog scent
she's been busy brewing all spring
and half the summer, rolling in
the devil only knows what all.

I tried the tub, but add a dog to water
and there's a powerful chemical reaction.
Some canine element starts everything shaking
and the whole wet works can blow up in your face,

which it turns out is a pretty efficient way
to spray-paint your bathroom walls, but
it's a damned odd-smelling primer,
and you sure won't want a second coat.

So I gave the downstairs shower a try,
dropped a plastic screen over the drain,
but it doesn't take much to flood a basement floor,
some tufts of hair, a blade of grass or three,

and while I was busy cursing, cleaning out the screen,
my four-legged, dripping-wet sponge was skating
down the hall and up the stairs,
for one long bone-jarring shudder at the top,

before quick-skittering through the kitchen
to drop and roll on the living room rug,
as though it represented something faintly
and rather suspiciously familiar.

Anyway, these days, bath-time for Smokie
means we're headed for the river or the hose.

A Different Taste in Literature

Guess I'll have to order another copy of Mike's book.
It had a cover when I borrowed it, and should probably
have one when I give it back. It looks somewhat naked
at the moment, and a bit ravaged with the cover gone,
ragged pieces of it strewn about the living room rug.

It's just the latest in a series of such misdemeanors,
and there's ample evidence available for determining
the culprit's identity. As a matter of fact, I'd wager
I could find her right now laying low somewhere, say
out back scattering that pile of leaves I just got raked together.

Save Your Breath (for the dance)

Family often told my brother-in-law
smoking like he did would one day kill him.
Good advice, but it soured fast—
the more they preached, the more he smoked
to make it clear to one and all
it was his life and he'd live it his way.
And he did, by god, and it killed him.
But everybody's gotta die somehow.

When it was her time to go, Mom
told me to look after my diabetic brother
who'd made it clear he didn't want any help,
though while she lived she kept on trying.
So I told her I would, and I did I guess,
those times I could, when his blood sugar fell
so low he no longer recognized
who was handing him the fix.

And maybe it was that childhood warning—
never take candy from a stranger—
but at times he'd take a swing at me,
and I'd hold his arms down and we'd stumble around
to the wild music of our barking dogs
confused by the scene—him cursing, me laughing,
leading my brother in a drunken dance
while a Snickers bar, his favorite, did its slow work.

Because

Each autumn she runs the yucca-clustered hills,
this ancient grassland full of prickly pear and prairie rose,
ranging ahead, casting left and right,
reveling in the scents, as meadowlarks
and mourning doves lift up and out of reach,
deer and coyotes slip away unseen,
and jackrabbits challenge her to open-country races
we all three know she can't win, but
know too she has to follow, because

out here, away from the common
chaos of the streets in the city where we live,
she can hear again a voice within
calling her back to her birthright,
the uncluttered wild, where everything is
a simple coupling, predator and prey,
every scent a call to grace—Follow me—
and nose down, tail aquiver,
without question she obeys, because

this way is narrow and she knows
it leads to the holy of holies,
the eternal present, where she locks on point,
silent, motionless, eye-to-eye,
pointer and sharptail a single being
lost in timeless meditation
before the inevitable sacrifice—
a grouse bursts skyward, my dog leaps after,
and I wake from this trance and raise the gun, because

Wolf-Song Heart

in memory of Louis Owens

Behind my aging dog this evening,
I watch her thinning, wire-haired body
scuttle down the bike trail south of town,
heading west in her angular trot
past harrowed fields of corn stubble,
stout wind dusting the tin-gray sky,
trees along the trail just starting to bud.

She slips into last year's knee-high grass
along the shoulder and fades from sight
like her namesake, Smoke, then reappears
tracking something in the fence-line brush
to a sudden point where she drops and rolls—
Let it be, I yell in her direction, but
she emerges chewing on a scrap of deer-hide.

And I can't help smiling, unable to conceal
my respect for her immediate response to hunger,
echo of that still-wild song in her heart
ringing out here in the open air, where
the eternal pulse of life-and-death
reflects an enigma far beyond
the sorely stunted range of human diction.

And though I realize these odd black marks
must fall as short as a novice newsman's
attempt to convey a sense of hurricane
from a desk in sunny Iowa, here
where the praises of prairie wolves still
echo down the heart of Mystery,
I've found my personal Savior.

Old Habits

Into the blossoming essence of April,
my twelve-year-old dog leads me out to the trestle,
and we head west between white-flowered thickets,
the wild plums abloom either side of the trail.

Unleashed at last from the day's cares, I run
out of old habit, like a dog in a dream
tracking down a long-gone litter of pups and
fetching them back one or two at a time—

Happy and Lucky, Tiny and Snowball,
Willie and Nikki, Kelly and Ace,
Pee-Wee, both Peppers (one spotted, one black),
Fred and Barney, Duke, the two Belles,

Cory, Yoda, Rowdy, Rusty,
Rocky, Aries, Aspen and Trey,
Mattie, Emmet, Jenny, Blizzard,
Buddy, the Gypsy—each of them rare,

a perfect misfit in a misshapen pack
of pedigreed pointers, coonhounds, retrievers,
a cross-bred assortment of happenchance mutts,
howlers and barkers, bay-ers, yarkers,

beggars and stealers, old lollygaggers,
bold tail-sniffers, wild trouble-makers,
loafers and tireless pissers of tires,
each without question a best-friend for life.

Out to the feedlot and back to the trestle,
trailing Smoke, the living heart of the pack,
I hear in the blossoming rasp of her panting
the approach of the dreamer that will fetch us all home.

Going, Going . . .

Smoke 1995-2013, thanks to Louise and Dr. Torkelson,
Dr. Stephenson, Dr. Brauer, and a Happy pup

I thought jealousy might do my old dog in,
until a friend and colleague told me
a pup just might keep her going.
And sure enough, Louise was right—
by the time that pup turned one year old
Smoke had put another year behind her.

Every morning, true to her namesake,
Happy'd start jacking around in the yard,
circling Smoke, just out of reach,
barking, growling, trying to tempt her
into endless games of Catch me if you can!

And that seemed to help Smoke limber up
those stiff hind legs each morning, lunging
and snapping until sooner or later
with a short yelp of shock, Happy'd agree
it was time to settle down.

Thanks to three veterinarians and that pup,
Smoke spent seventeen years on the planet,
slow, but steady as the Energizer Bunny,
beat cancer twice after Happy showed up,
tumors so aggressive they quickly grew
themselves to death and drained away.

Stiff as a dry pine board some mornings,
she still came fully alive in the field,
hunting, pointing, swimming any water
at the grand old age of seventeen, this
mysterious being bringing me to believe
no one short of God has the means to measure

any living entity's capacity for heart.

Attempt to Share What Cannot Be Shared

"In my Father's house…" John 14:2

If I told you the width of the gap she once cleared
you wouldn't believe it, just as I wouldn't have
if I hadn't seen it that September day—
the sharptail falling and a quick brown blur
streaking toward it through thigh-high grass
to the edge of an incredible span.

Though she's gone now, I can still see it,
like a photo series there wasn't time to graph,
and here, without suitably accurate means
to convey the inexplicable power and grace
that lifted and carried her over that gulf,
I defer to your creativity.

Imagine a Drahthaar running flat out
to the lip of a blowout she can't see until
she's all at once airborne and over…and
the heart that lifted her there must live on
in memory, or imagination,
or another such mansion in the house of God.

Naming Dogs:
Intrusions of Memory in 20 Sonnets

Cat Man

The dogs and I pass the Cats and cranes
rebuilding one of half a dozen bridges
lost to the flooding river this spring,
and I can hear my uncle forty years ago,

That's the damnedest idea I ever heard—
straightening the river to save farms upstream.
They're just speeding it up. A big flood
now'll tear hell out of everything.

Cat jockey the better part of his life,
something he learned back in the army,
Wayne pushed dirt for ditches and dams
on irrigation projects throughout the Midwest.
And though he never lived to see that flood,
he knew damned well what he was talking about.

1

My two Drahthaars dance and whine until
I open the door of my Mercury and
they're off, nosing into autumn bluestem
on this warm September afternoon.
It's the first trip to the field for the pup,
time to see what she can learn from Smoke.

Spring Lakes my uncle called this place
that May some fifty years ago
when he stopped by the playground at recess
to see if I wanted to ride along.
The carp were up from the river, spawning.
So I skipped school and the rest of the day
watched my uncle, tall as Poseidon,
gigging fish with a home-made spear.

2

The dogs emerge on a hillock of oaks,
an odd, isolated stand of trees
rising like some island paradise
out of this sea of chest-high grass.
From a deer trail halfway up the mound,
I spot a monarch overhead, then
hundreds, flickering, animate leaves
lighting up the canopy above.

Any time a job was close enough
he could work the day and drive us back,
Wayne took my brother and me along.
Once, we each caught a limit of catfish
from an irrigation ditch east of Monroe
while he pushed dirt for berms with a Cat.

3

I follow the pup, and she follows Smoke,
moving south now out of the oaks and
across a swale to what was once riverbank.
As we skirt the slough below the bluff
a great blue heron lifts from the shallows
and slowly wings away to the east.

I was ten, Joel twelve, that summer
Wayne handed each of us a beer
as we roared back to Stanton in his beat-up Ford
after he'd worked the day on the Sherman dam.
And along the Elkhorn south of Beemer
he shared the sandwiches he'd brought for lunch,
his mother's fresh bread, home-made catsup,
and farm-fresh, fried-in-bacon-grease eggs.

4

At the west edge of the shallow slough
the dogs move slower, working their way
through a patch of sandburs, until the pup
pulls up, sits down among the burs, then
flops onto her belly to gnaw at those
stuck between the pads of her big front paws.

One time, the weather too wet to work,
Wayne took us to the river and showed us how
he'd string a length of chicken gut onto a wire
with a loop at one end, slip a hook through the loop,
then slide the gut up onto the line,
anchor it with a half-hitch at the top,
and knot the tail end around the hook,
so the fish, feeling nothing sharp, would swallow.

5

I look for a safe place to kneel
and help the pup pull burs from her feet.
When she rises at last and shakes herself,
I stand, look across the water and see
some half-dozen V-shaped waves, big carp,
and once more I picture Wayne with his spear.

He always searched out the deepest holes,
and usually hooked a big catfish or two,
while Joel and I caught some smaller ones
off the bare sandbars or grassy banks
where we fished to avoid the mosquito clouds
that rose from the brush Wayne waded through,
the gnats always bad enough, swarming in
as soon as we opened a jar of those guts.

6

Across the slough a lone Canada goose
swims slowly toward a thick stand of reeds,
having lost its mate perhaps, though I notice
the fist-sized head of a snapping turtle
surface in the shallows on the other side.
I've seen other geese missing a foot.

One day, Wayne came out of the brush with no fish,
said, "We gotta go," and pointed southwest
at thick, green cloud billows in the sky.
The rain hit as we got in his pickup,
an old GMC with steering so loose
he had to spin the wheel full around, then back,
to stay on the crown of the muddy road
as we raced that turquoise mass toward town.

7

Half a dozen wood ducks whistle in
from the east and circle the slough
until they see me or the dogs, then flare,
retreating to a farther stretch of water,
another piece of this spring-fed puzzle,
where they all cup wings and drop from sight.

Back in Norfolk, we made it inside
before the big hailstones started to rattle,
knocking out windows, denting siding,
battering roofs all over town.
Later that summer, as he shingled our house,
Joel and me helping where we could,
Wayne told us it was his second time—
"I helped your dad when he built this place."

8

Smoke, sixteen now, takes to the water,
out of the burs and the tangles of brush
on the bank, but the pup, four months old,
forges ahead until she finds
a faint trail in the face of the bluff,
a grassed-over crevice not overly steep,
where the three of us converge and start
to climb what was once the bank of the river.

I can't recall Wayne taking anyone
but Joel and me along to fish on those
water projects he worked close to home,
though he had two daughters about the same
ages then as my brother and me,
and a son just a few years younger.

9

The dogs make their separate ways up the bluff,
the pup lunging ahead, Smoke trotting behind.
And I trail them until we reach the top,
then call them in, so we can rest a bit
while I check their paws and make sure
they're free of burs and ready to start
the next leg of this excursion,
working our way back down to the car.

Maybe taking us fishing when he could,
re-roofing our house after the hail,
were ways Wayne found to honor our father,
a man thirty years older than himself, and
from stories he later shared with me,
in some ways like a dad to him.

10

When the dogs get restless, ready to move,
I turn and look back down from the bluff
at the slough and the river far beyond,
this piece of earth Wayne shared with me
that spring some fifty years ago
and every season I've come here since.

And maybe he felt he couldn't fail with us,
as it seemed he had with his own family,
since no one could rightly expect him to care.
But to us each trip with Wayne was a gift,
and back then he was the only one giving.
Forget "visit the fatherless and widows,"
the church that excommunicated him,
and later me, never offered one damn thing.

11

From this perspective, atop the bluff,
I can see a dark mass off to my left,
high in a cottonwood towering up
from the ancient riverbank below,
an aerie of woven sticks, vacant now,
though I once saw fledglings in another.

I recall the farm Wayne had early on,
the pasture and woodlot, barn and sheds,
playing with our cousins in the weed-choked fields
he somehow never found time to work.
Once, he saw me with a slingshot and said
barn swallows got that name from taking
tornadoes by the tail and swallowing them whole
to protect their nests under the eaves of barns.

12

The pup hangs back as Smoke starts stalking
something in a stand of cedars on the bluff,
slowly, quietly, out of the sunlight
into the dappled shadows. Though dark
as this pup when my nephew named her,
Smoke's wire-hair has gone mostly white,
the thick tufts paled and curled with age,
now resembling wisps of her namesake.

Once, after a warning on the radio,
my aunt called us kids down to the cellar,
Wayne off in town again, I guess.
When I tried to assure them that we'd be safe,
and told them how barn swallows got that name,
I found no one else would swallow that story.

13

I follow the dogs as they move west,
skirting some poison ivy under the trees,
into an open stretch of Sandhills,
short summer grasses, yuccas, wild rose.
Another hundred yards and we swing north
past a blowout full of cast-off yesterdays,
rusted-through machinery, old bedsprings,
a sturdy, though not quite bullet-proof range,
jagged pieces of jars and bottles,
a scattered wealth of antique junk.

Good at fishing, pushing dirt with a Cat,
not much at farming, even less at being
husband and father when he wasn't on the road,
Wayne was our family's black sheep, I guess.

14

As we work our way down a long grass slope,
I can see the gravel road ahead,
and on the wide oak ridge beyond,
too far for the dogs to pick up scent,
three deer grow nervous and spin around,
white tails flashing back into the trees.

He liked whiskey, poker, running wild,
perhaps not strange, growing up in a bar,
learning early on how to live alone. Yet
before things got so bad he lost the farm
and took up again what he'd learned in the army,
moving tons of dirt day-to-day with a Cat,
Wayne had two dogs he called Happy and Lucky,
named I suppose for what he felt at the time.

15

The dogs slip under a falling-down fence,
and I step over into un-grazed pasture,
starting another swing, to the east this time,
as we circle down toward the Mercury,
avoiding the poison ivy on the bluff,
those sandburs along the trail behind.

I know now he was a contradiction,
leaving his family time and again,
yet somehow sharing with my brother and me
a reverential love for places like this.
No matter what else he was, he was
the closest thing we had to a father,
aged five and eight when our dad died,
and that's something I will not forget.

16

Nose down, stalking a grassed-over ditch,
Smoke takes a final step and locks up.
Spotting her, the curious pup soon lopes
into a raucous burst of color,
a rooster pheasant cackling skyward
after flushing a foot from the old dog's nose.

The last time I came here with Wayne,
it was the spring spawn, I had a fishing bow,
and he stood watching from the road
as I waded the slough and shot four carp.
I remembered that May thirty years before,
him spearing carp, three gunny sacks full.
When I took him back to the Center,
I gave him the two biggest fish.

17

Full circle now, almost back to the bluestem,
I can see the car beyond the dogs.
Smoke's wearing down, falling back with me,
But the pup's fired up, working left and right,
nose to the ground some twenty yards out,
looking almost perfect. I can't help but grin.

Year after year, through the warmer months
Wayne left town and followed the jobs,
returning each winter to wait for spring,
when the dirt-work crews would gather again.
But in the end, age brought him back
to the town and the bar where he'd been raised,
and family now gone their separate ways,
he could reflect on the long, wild run he'd made.

18

A year ago a friend and I spotted a pup
in the ditch on a remote gravel road.
He was skinny, sickly, but when we stopped the car
he came up to her, little tail wagging.
She wasn't sure about a stray at first,
but he's healthy now, and he was
easy to name—we just called him Lucky.

The dogs move close now, through the tall grass.
They can't see the car, but Smoke knows where it is,
and Happy, falling in behind, will learn.
In time, like Smoke, she'll understand
as soon as I open the car door,
no matter where we start, we'll always be
circling, taking the long way home.

The Hard Way

The Happy Dog heads for a lone red cedar,
one of some dozen eight-foot mavericks
scattered about this patch of virgin prairie.
She's learned to take a break when hunting grouse.

I follow her, fill a small bowl with water
from one of the four pints I carry now
on these early-September afternoons.
Wire-haired pointers will hunt until they drop.

When her panting slows she laps up a drink,
then stretches flat-out on her belly
on the shaded side of the tree.
She knows we'll wait until she's ready to go.

I once carried Smoke a quarter mile
to a Sandhills pond. And she lived. And I learned.

Other Dogs

Lucky

Skinny gray pup
in a grassed-over ditch
along a county road,
he looked at first
to be a coyote.

Shepherd mix
with a sweet disposition,
sleek, lean, and born to run,
before age took his hips
it seemed he had wings.

Flushing grouse
in open country
he'd flat-out streak after
tight as a shadow
for a hundred yards.

Gone now from this
corporeal plane,
he's still running, I know,
faster than ever—at last
he can out-and-out fly.

At Blue Hole

Autumn wind ripped yellow leaves off
cottonwoods surrounding the long pit
where I bent low and he crouched at heel,
stalking the little raft of teal.

They flushed, I shot and two birds fell.
He lunged for the nearest and
brought in the drake while the south wind
carried the hen away from shore.

Out again but not far enough,
he turned to me and I signaled,
sorry when he circled and swam on,
too far I thought for a half-grown pup.

Going out was easy, riding the waves,
but when he picked her up and came around
he faced the wind and the long way back,
and I cursed—he seemed to be swimming in place.

Then he was coming, plodding
but gaining, and I was walking out,
something inside pulling, knowing
part of the heart that would bring him in was mine.

When his feet touched bottom and he shook himself,
he nearly fell in the shallow water, and his tail
began that timeless dance as he dropped the warm
blue-wing in my trembling hand.

Brothers

for Dave

We crossed the frozen channel in the dark,
set out decoys and huddled in the blind
over coffee and the Coleman stove,
hunting a last time together,
no mention of your separation,
not a word about impending divorce,
the young Lab shaking wild between us
as dawn flowered like blood on water,
drawing black lines of geese along the river.

They were high and stayed up,
the day clear and cold, but we hunkered
until dark on the frozen river,
brothers in a more natural sense than law,
shivering with the dog when the stove went out,
watching the sky and calling, calling,
all that long day on the Platte,
waiting for something, a straggler, a loner,
for one last shot before the light ran out.

Some Nights

A year-old pup in a cattail slough, he climbs
thin air after a cackling pheasant,
comes down with his mouth full of feathers,
eyes so wild he could fly away with the bird.

Dark as midnight, glistening, he swims again
the long pit, across the icy water and back
against the wind with the crippled teal,
something struggling to get away in his eyes.

And some nights I hunt the field alone,
out to the road where he lies, black
as silence in the ditch, and his eyes
tell me he knows what is stalking us all.

Friends

—in memory of Gary Lee Entsminger
for Susan

My first writing teacher was a backpacker,
and we hiked into Wyoming wilderness,
fished unnamed lakes, ate mountain trout,
canoed various wild rivers for miles,
drank and argued and laughed together
over Blake, Tennyson, Yeats, works of art,
friends for nearly 20 years, before
Larry died on a Nebraska highway
with the new Lab pup he'd named Hershey.

From the Castle on a Colorado mountain
Gary sent tales and photographs
of his adventures with Susan,
hiking, gardening, publishing
exquisite literature and art,
and I knew I'd found familiar friends, but
before we had the chance to meet,
Gary died of an aneurysm
a few months after losing his Lab, Garcia.

The too-sudden loss of friends feels both
tragic and inevitable,
this planet forever a mystery,
offering the most precious gifts
for what always seems too short a time,
leaving mere ghosts, these memories, yet
each is part of that ancient enigma
the earliest people understood
to be God.

Three Dogs

Driving south through the reservation,
I saw what looked like three dogs resting
on the shoulder of the gravel road ahead.

I stopped, got out, and three heads turned,
two large dogs and a yearling doe,
dark blood and bits of flesh on the snow,
the deer's hindquarters eaten half away.

Three wary sets of eyes watched me
get the lug wrench from the trunk.

When I walked toward her, the crippled doe,
utterly calm a moment before,
lurched in panic, trying to drag
those mangled haunches that anchored her.

The dogs got up and slinked away
as I swung the iron and crushed her skull,
telling myself it was the proper thing,
freeing her from that slow death.

But I can't forget how still she lay,
wholly resigned to her gruesome fate,
until she somehow sensed the darkness gnawing
inside me as I approached.

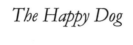

The Happy Dog

This Dog Hunts

She lies in the shade west of the garage,
scanning the sky, scenting the morning,
out on the lawn I mowed yesterday
before our run down the hike-and-bike trail,

that section closed now after the flood,
where I turned her loose as a wish on the world,
and she sprinted down the nearly unmarred trail,
everything erased by last night's rain

except a few fresh tracks of deer and coyote,
and no doubt those pheasants she pushed off the trail
and burrowed through the waist-high grass to point,
before my approach sent them clawing skyward.

But it's September now, and all she wants
is to be out there, because…

All the Way

Blackbirds, robins, and rabbits scatter
each spring morning as the Happy Dog bounds
out the back door and into the yard
to secure her familiar perimeter.

Back inside, after a hearty breakfast,
it's onto the couch, rooting and scooting
the throw pillows onto the floor before
she curls up and gives a great sigh of relief.

Eight years old she remains the pup
I know she will be till the end.
Smoke and the Gypsy played and hunted,
excited as ever, both seventeen,
each still conjuring the spirit of youth
all the too-short way to her grave.

Morning Meditation

At the kitchen window
I'm sipping coffee and watching
a half-grown rabbit munch clover
a few short hops from the gate.

Then I see the Happy Dog's
glacial inching toward the trespasser,
as patient as Job
stalking his God.

Across the River to the Underworld

When I quit fishing and call,
her barking seems a long way off,
until I discover it echoes
from a fist-sized hole in the bank.

I splash toward the sound,
and belly-deep in the river
paw at the packed mud and sand
of a caved-in beaver run.

In time I grab her collar,
digging with my other hand,
the opening at last wide enough
I can drag her out of the dark.

No! I yell, slapping at her
again and again until her patient gaze
brings me back from the hole in the earth
I dug for Smokie three months ago.

Shake, Rattle and Roll

The Happy Dog rides shotgun as we head out to water the horses
on my friend's place over by Hadar, where I figure she can
get some exercise while the tank fills and I walk the fence,
making sure the hot-wire throws a fair spark,
pulling up the odd thistle here and there.

Halfway across the pasture I see her stop and sniff the ground,
and I start yelling but I can see it's too damn late—
she flops down and rolls in something I know long before
I pick up the scent is gonna be rank as raw sewage
in spite of her acting like they oughtta bottle the stuff.

Sure enough, back at the car—Sweet Jesus!—that's nothing I want
the horses drinking, so we head for the nearest other water,
the North Fork roiling with last night's rain, where after a good dip
she still smells short of the proverbial rose, so back home
I hook up the hose and we work on a livable compromise.

At last I nod and turn off the water, then stand there dripping
as I watch her wild, wire-haired method of drying off—
after a mighty full-body shake, she dives nose-first
into the grass and starts root-and-rolling in such a way
it brings a certain old rock-and-roll classic to mind.

The Happy Dog Horks Down a Whole Damn Chicken

Each year my friend Ken heads up to the Hutterite colony
in South Dakota to buy dressed chickens for himself and others,
so he calls me up last June and asks if I want some, and I say
"Sure. I'll take five for myself and a couple for friends."

So, seven chickens on the way, I go downstairs
to check the freezer for space, and damn—I still got three
from last year I kinda forgot about, and I figure I'd better
get 'em eaten, so I take one upstairs and put it in the sink
to thaw while I head over to Lou's for some fixins.

Well, I'm gone fifteen minutes at most, but when I get back,
there's no chicken in the sink, and there's only one reason
I can think of, so I look around and sure enough,
there's the plastic the chicken came in, beside a thumbnail-size
bit of bone and a chicken-size wet spot on the couch,
and that's it, that's all that's left of a 4-pound bird.

I call the Happy Dog, who's slinked off somewhere, and when she
shows up I can see she's swelled up fat as a full-blown tick,
and I start to worry she might up and croak, so I load her in the car
and head for the country, thinking a run might do her some good,
and it does, I guess, 'cuz after a mile or so on the Cowboy Trail
and two or three healthy deposits, she seems okay, and we head back.

I open the car-door and she jumps in, onto the backseat just in time
to chuck up what remains of that chicken on the floor of my Mercury.
And I end a robust round of cursing with thanks to gas-stop eateries
for the napkins of various pedigrees I find scattered about the car.
Then I start cleanin', 'cuz I've had dogs enough to know if I don't
what's left a' that chicken's gonna get re-cycled
and we can start the whole process over again.

Well, I get it done and re-load the Happy Dog, who's shrunk some now,
almost back to her fit-and-trim self, and a couple of old proverbs
come to mind—All's well that ends well, and Happy is as Happy does.
But a whole damn chicken! Jesus! It ain't like I don't feed her.
What the hell's she thinking?

Leggin' & Beggin'

A friend sends an email advertising residencies
for poets and writers at a farmhouse in Tennessee,
where if you qualify you get a private room,
office space with wireless internet, cable,
and use of a communal kitchen.

Obviously a great deal for the unencumbered,
but these days I travel with the Happy Dog,
and I can already imagine her avid attempts
to commune with our colleagues in that kitchen.

The Happy Dog Up and Upchucks a Woodchuck

I hear her gag, glance over
and see the odd remains
issue from her mouth
like some alien birth—

a mass of innards
in a mess of brown hair
I can't identify until
she exits the woodpile
a short while later,

and as she prances happily by,
mouthing a familiar-hued beast
limp as an old boot,
I holler, "Drop that critter!"
and she actually does.

In Poor Taste

I'm enjoying a cold Heineken
when I notice my Drahthaar begin
to gag, and then upchuck
half a damn woodchuck,
and that beer just don't taste quite the same.

After Watching a Documentary on Wolves

A determined paw thumps the bed beside me,
a degree less traumatic though nearly as effective
as a drill sergeant hollering, First call! while
hammering a baton against a metal trashcan.

It's the Happy Dog's morning wake-up,
and I'm well aware it will reoccur
at sporadic intervals until I rise, but
this ain't the army, so I go on feigning sleep.

On third call, I obey the summons, get up, dress,
and head for the kitchen to scare up her breakfast—
two large scoops from a can of Alpo Prime Cuts
and a couple of full cups of kibble.

By the time I get the coffee going, she's already
sniffing out dessert, eyes locked on the refrigerator,
where I get out a chunk of hamburger
and watch something inside her awaken.

It brings to mind last night's film on wolves,
where a pack took down a full-grown elk,
and each member glutted itself after the kill.
I can see it in the Happy Dog's eyes right now—
Come on, man! Let's eat the whole damn cow!

Trademark

Twice I've stitched her myself,
once stapled a five-inch gash,
but now there's a sizeable piece
of wire-haired hide flapping at her side,
so I call the Happy Dog to heel,
and it's back to the car and into town
for her first overnight stay at the vet's.

Early next morning I pick her up,
check out where they shaved her side,
cut away the loose strip of skin
and sewed her tough hide back together
with a dozen big, lumped stitches resembling
those on some old moccasin.

She seems no worse for the odd new wear,
just another day outdoors for her, running
across one of the hazards of her trade,
though this one's gonna leave a definite mark.

A Walk Along the River

A February afternoon, fifty degrees,
perfect time, I thought, to take the dog
for a walk at the wildlife management area.
Runoff had flooded the access trail,
so I parked on high ground near the road,
crossed the running water in a narrow place,
and headed north, the dog running
parallel to me through a stand of trees,
where a crippled doe broke from the brush.

The dog took chase, and I yelled "No!" but
she was over the bank and into the water,
and before I could tear through the brambles between us
they were halfway across the river.
I yelled again, though I knew it was useless,
the dog I'd brought for a walk was gone,
lost somewhere way back in time,
where a wild predator was locked on prey
somewhere near three times her size,
barking, lunging and snapping at the neck,
the deer slashing out with sharp front hooves,
trying to knock her away or push her under,
and both of them moving away with the current
toward fallen trees in the bend ahead.

Running the bank as they rode the river,
I was trying to keep close enough to reach the dog
if they swept into a snag and she went under,
but they were in the channel and I was losing ground,
the current straight now, picking up speed,
as I ran into mud and fell farther behind.
When they went into the next wide bend,
I was slogging through backwater shallows,
crossing a half-submerged beaver dam,
then climbing the eight-foot riverbank
into another thicket where they both
went out of sight as I attempted to pinpoint
the direction of the barking in case it stopped.

Then I saw the doe in the middle of the river,
the dog farther on, caught in the current,
trying to swim upstream, but drifting
away from the now-stationary deer
and toward a long downfall in the water.
"Here!" I yelled as I stumbled from the brush,
signaling with my arm to turn toward the bank,
until I saw her swing my way and somehow
paddle past the deadfall into shallow water.
I watched the doe standing motionless
in ripples over a submerged sandbar,
until the dog got close enough to grab
by the scruff and pull away from the water,
out of sight of the deer so she wouldn't start again.
Through the thicket and down the high bank,
I crossed the beaver dam again, then stopped,
the dog no longer showing interest.

The deer was still standing out there in the water,
and by now odds were she wouldn't make it out.
They'd battled for almost a mile on the river,
each of them trying to put the other down,
and the doe clearly crippled from the start.
I waited, watching, hoping she'd move,
but each time she tried, she seemed to lose her balance.
I thought she was just too weak at the time,
but I wonder now if she'd stood too long,
slowly sinking in that loose, wet sand until,
with just three legs, she couldn't pull herself out.

The water around her was the color of sky,
a darker blue in the ripples where she stood,
the colors all grown oddly bright
as they do when the day approaches dusk.
On the bank above, young cottonwoods
stretched bone-white against the woods beyond,
and farther north, on the cemetery hill,
little mounds of snow hung on beneath the cedars.
I turned and walked the dog back out to the car.

This Animal

She pounces and chews on a tennis ball
when I kneel on the rug in the living-room
to stretch my legs before our morning run
along the river on the new bike trail
they poured over the defunct U. P. line,
where she'll head west along the right-of-way
and I'll follow, conscious of her leading me
out of complacence and once again
into a world she can sense somehow
still blooming at the end of that ancient track,
and I know if I let her take me back,
let the rotten fruits of knowledge fall
like crusted scales from a blind man's eyes,
I'll be with her today in paradise.

Lone Companions

As a boy I had a stuffed brown dog
with a stubby tail and floppy ears,
a gift from German grandparents,
my lone companion when in trouble,
a rather frequent occurrence back then.

Since that time I've had three
German wire-haired pointers, each
brown, with a short tail and floppy ears,
and each a gift from a different person
unfamiliar with my younger years.

Up on the Pine Ridge, out in the Sandhills,
on the Elkhorn, Niobrara, Loup, and Platte,
Gypsy, Smokie, Happy and me shared
numerous joys and sorrows on our adventures
mining the remnants of Eden.

Some still treat dogs like implements,
tools to use when convenient, or toys
to play with until tired, then put away.
But nothing outside these lone companions
ever drew me nearer my God to Thee.

She Died on the Bed that Night

Through the kitchen window I can see
the neighbor's dead willow that two weeks ago
nearly took out my garage. I'm looking out
to avoid looking down
at the Happy Dog licking her right rear leg
and the gaping sore that must be more cancer,
no doubt having spread from the mass on her lung,
her nose already nearly swollen shut.

There's really not much left of her now,
a wire-haired skeleton sporadically bleeding
on the kitchen floor, where pots and plates
with the food I've left grow brown and dry,
untouched, and still she refuses to give it up,
the connection we've shared these past ten years.

Staring at her, I'm awed at the strength still present
in the heart of this animal that will not release me
from the walk we must take in the morning,
the last adventure we will share.

For the Love of God

Whether I was gone fifteen minutes or half a day,
she met me at the door, mouthing a toy and growling low,
tail pumping like I'd been gone for weeks. For ten years
she was the Happy Dog, and she was mine. Then she was gone.

In my experience, the companionship of a dog is as close
as a human being can come to unconditional love on this planet.

And I curse the mentality that killed her, the godless idea
that profit somehow takes precedence over life and love,
sell-out governments allowing corporate interests to create
and disperse the deadly toxins that pollute earth, water, and air.

This corporate mentality is killing the planet, creature by creature.
And for the love of God, it's time to wake up and end it.

Eve of the Winter Solstice

Two nights past full, the moon climbs
a cloudless sky as Orion rises.
Between them, in Canis Major,
Sirius, Earth's brightest star, known
to cultures as disparate as those of ancient
China, Assyria, and various peoples
of North America, by names that translate to
Dog Star, Wolf Star, Moon Dog.

Legend in India calls this star, Svana,
the faithful dog of Prince Yudhishthira,
and in time his lone companion on the search
for heaven, where they're told dogs are not allowed.
But when they both turn to leave, the guard calls them back
and ushers them through the gate together.

About the Author

Neil Harrison's poetry collections include *In a River of Wind* (Bridge Burner's Publishing 2000), *Into the River Canyon at Dusk* (Lone Willow Press 2005), *Back in the Animal Kingdom* (Pinyon Publishing 2011), and *Where the Waters Take You* (Pinyon Publishing 2018), winner of a 2019 Nebraska Center for the Book Honor Award. A former instructor of English and Creative Writing, he lives in Northeast Nebraska.

CPSIA information can be obtained
at www.ICGtesting.com
Printed in the USA
JSHW020929170523
41820JS00004B/28